DOCKSIDE

STAGE **6** BOOK 5

BREAKABLE

John Townsend

RISING ★ STARS

Nadia was giving a first aid lesson at Club OK.
She was showing what to do if someone breaks a leg.
Gavin was her model.

"Come on, Gavin, you're very sensible. Make your leg look like it's broken. You play lots of sport so your leg should be flexible," she said.

Gavin smiled as he lay on the floor and twisted his leg.

"Anything's possible, Nadia," he said. "In fact, I once broke my leg in two places – once on the rugby field and again in the dressing room when I fell off the stretcher!"

They all laughed.

4

Nadia showed them how to use a splint to keep a broken leg straight.

"Use something suitable like a stick or a broom handle as a splint. Use whatever is available. It keeps the leg still and comfortable while we wait for the ambulance to arrive," she said.

Gavin giggled, "I've got a terrible itch and I can't scratch it now."
They all laughed again.

"I'm going to show you what to do if someone stops breathing. It was once called *the kiss of life*," Nadia said.

Gavin sat up with a smile, "Really, Nadia?"

"Don't worry, Gavin. Although you're adorable, I'm going to use the lovely Annie." Nadia put a dummy on the floor.

Spod called out, "Why is she called Annie and not Anna? She looks like my sister."
Anna laughed, "But at least I'm breathing!"

They took turns to try their first aid skills on Annie. They had to blow into her mouth and also keep her heart beating.

"One day you may have to help someone like this," Nadia said. "So you're learning a valuable lesson tonight."

When they had finished the lesson, Nadia asked Anna to pack the dummy away.

"Can you take Annie out to my car and sit her in the front seat? You should be able to find my car out there in the dark! Thanks, Anna," she said.

"Don't worry, Nadia. My sister is very reliable," Spod grinned.

Soon after Anna had gone,
JJ rushed in.
"Sorry I'm late," he panted.
He looked at his watch.
"That's incredible! I got
here on my skateboard in
under two minutes. Hey,
Spod, where's Anna?"

"She's putting something in Nadia's car," Spod said.

JJ went outside in the dark to find Anna. When he found Nadia's car, he opened the door. The light inside didn't work.

"Hi, Anna," he said. "Sorry I'm late. I had a horrible shock because my pet snake got out again. I found him in Dad's tool box hidden in all the wires and cables. He was almost invisible in all that lot!"

JJ had no idea he was talking to a dummy.

Anna came back indoors.

"Did you see JJ?" Spod asked.
"No," she said.
"Spod, can you take my
portable DVD player out
to my car for me, please?"
Nadia asked.

Spod came running back indoors with a big grin.

"Hey, come and look at this," he called. "You won't believe it. It's unbelievable! JJ is talking to Annie the dummy. He thinks she's Anna!"

Everyone rushed outside to look. Gavin ran ahead.

Gavin didn't see JJ's skateboard just outside the door. He got a horrible shock and landed with a crash. Nadia rushed to help him.

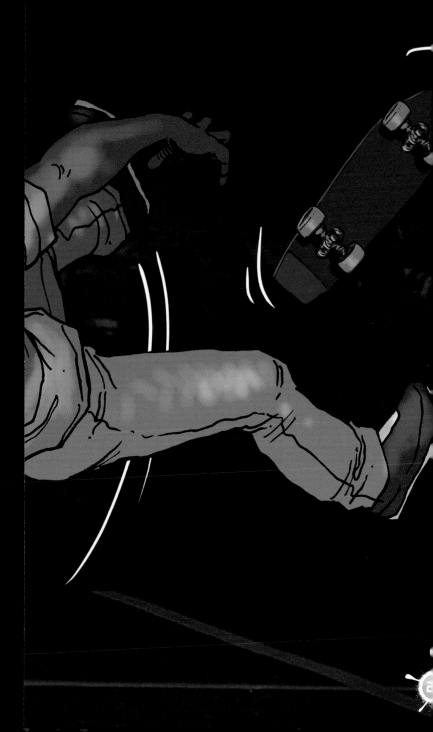

Gavin lay still on a stretcher when his mum and an ambulance arrived. "I think my leg's broken," he groaned. His mum sighed, "If anything is breakable, you can bet my Gavin will break it!"